MW01104808

"*Message in a Book* is a participatory medium for family, friends, and colleagues, to let them know how much they are loved and appreciated. Within our busy lives, it is easy to forget those most important. Michelle's concept will ignite a new way of boosting the morale of those most important in our lives. It will give a taste of positive encouragement — wholesome for both the sender and receiver of this unique book."

> — Arran Stephens, founder & president
> Nature's Path Foods Inc.

"What a wonderful way to touch the souls of others, and to send ripples of kindness out into the world. A unique concept, *Message in a Book* is bound to generate some interesting connecting and reflecting. People will have a lot of fun with this."

> — Gwen Randall-Young, psychotherapist and author of
> *Dancing Soul: The Voice of Spirit Evolving*
> *Echoes Through Time: A Message of Healing for Men*
> *Baby Soul: A Blessing of Spirit*

"It is vital to acknowledge people for who they are and what they have done. This book is stimulating me to write words that might otherwise have gone unspoken. The positive energy in *Message in a Book* will touch the lives of many people and let family and friends know how much they are loved."

> — Raymond L. Aaron,
> Canadian Business Coach,
> president The Raymond Aaron Group

Message in a Book

Making Connections
With People In Your Life

by
Michelle Patrizio

"I *know* that this book will bring many smiles
and much happiness to all who participate."

Canadian Cataloguing in Publication Data
Patrizio, Michelle, 1960-
Message in a book

ISBN 0-89716-839-9

1. Interpersonal Communication. 2. Blank-books.
I. Title.
CT9999.P37 1999   153.6   C99-910899-9

Editors: Suzanne Bastedo and Nancy Lewis
Text Design: Fiona Raven
Cover Design: Warren Denny

First printing August 1999

PEANUT BUTTER PUBLISHING
Suite 212 - 1656 Duranleau Street • Granville Island
• Vancouver, B.C. • Canada • V6H 3S4 • 604-688-0320 •
301-Pier 55, 1101 Alaskan Way • Seattle, WA 98101-2982
• 206-748-0345 •
email: pnutpubv@axion.net

Internet: http://www.pbpublishing.com

Printed in Canada

Acknowledgements

What started as an idea ... is now a reality. I would like
to thank all those who have helped me with *Message in a
Book*. The support and dedication of family, friends, and the
team at Peanut Butter Publishing have meant so very much
to me. Special appreciation to Peanut Butter's managing
editor, Jo Blackmore, who encouraged me to always put one
foot in front of the other, making this new experience
possible.

There are two ways of spreading light: to be
The candle or the mirror that reflects it.

Edith Wharton, *Artemis to Actaeon*, 1909

Imagine writing . . .

Imagine writing an inspiring message in a bottle and dropping it into the ocean. You watch the bottle float away, and know that someone, somewhere, will find your message and read it. They may be moved by your message, then add a message of their own and toss the bottle back into the water. Someday the message in the bottle may even find its way back to you! But from the time it leaves your hand, it is making a connection with whoever finds it.

Using
this book ...

Using this book is like writing a message in a bottle. On the first entry page, you write a message to someone in your life. Then you send or give the book to that person. She or he reads your message, then writes one to someone else on the next blank page, and passes the book on. The book is passed from person to person, acquiring more and more messages of support and appreciation. When it is full, it can be returned to the original sender as a treasure trove of mindfulness in everyday life!

You probably
know someone ...

You probably know someone you would really like to express your feelings to but haven't, for one reason or another. Maybe it's someone you haven't spoken with in a while, and you want to re-establish a meaningful connection. Maybe it's someone in your daily life whose actions you want to acknowledge. Maybe it's a stranger you've just met. Maybe your family or group wants to use *Message in a Book* to help celebrate a birthday, commemorate an anniversary, or mark some other special event.

Your message could be ...

Your message could be a note of appreciation, a special thank-you, a peace offering, a whimsical idea, a sentimental emotion . . . . Whether you've been wanting to say something for years, or express a feeling you're having right now, this book allows you to seize the moment and tell someone that you appreciate them in your life. Your words will join the messages that have been written before yours, and become part of an inspiring and ever-widening circle of connections.

It's easy
to pass the book on ...

It's easy to pass the book on! Just hand it to the person you've written the message to, or mail it to them. There is room for forty-eight messages. If you are the last person to write a message, please mail the book back to the publisher.

If you are
the original purchaser ...

If you are the original purchaser, please fill out the
enclosed postcard and mail it to Peanut Butter Publishing.

Each *Message in a Book* is assigned a unique serial number
which is on the postcard, on the part remaining attached to
the book, and on your own record. Thanks to the circle you
have initiated, this book will eventually be filled with
inspiring messages. By mailing the book back to the
publisher, the very last person to receive this book will
complete the circle.

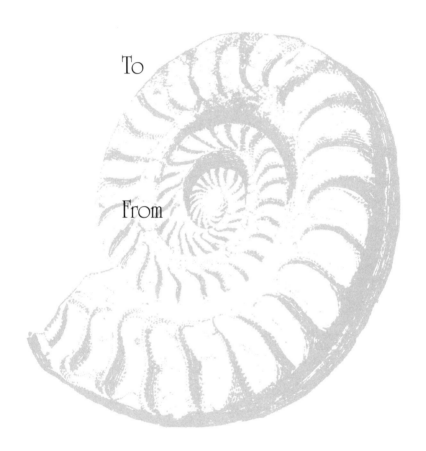

To

From

To

From

To

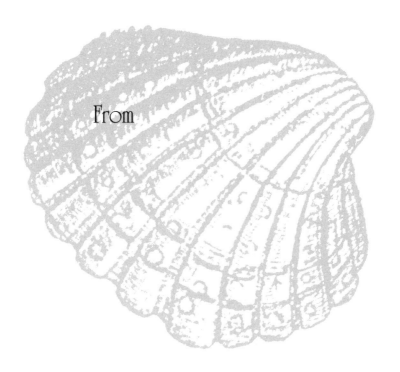

From

To

From

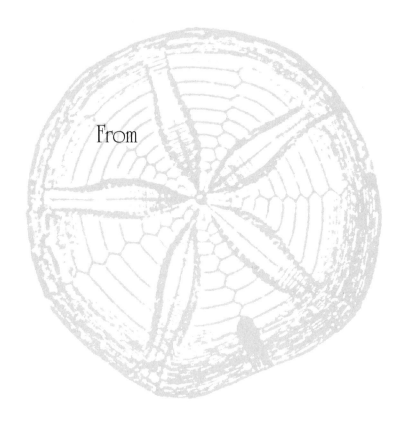

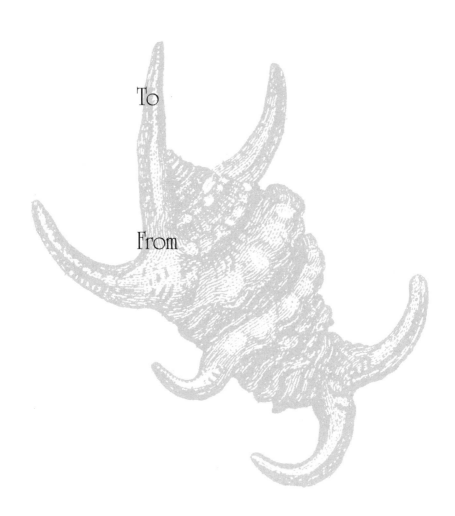

To

From

To

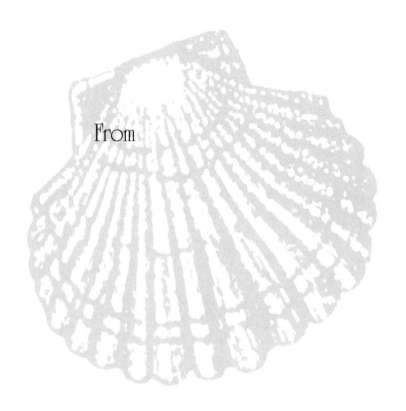

From

To

From

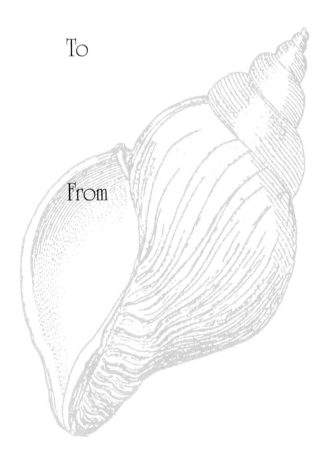

To

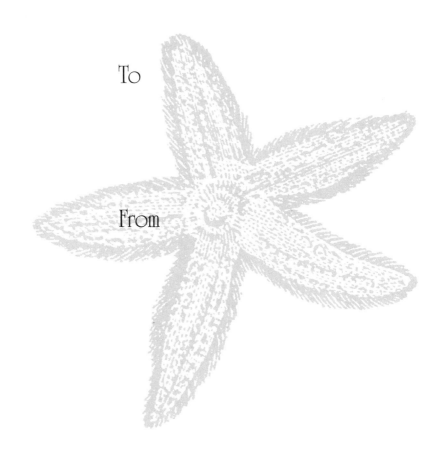

From

To

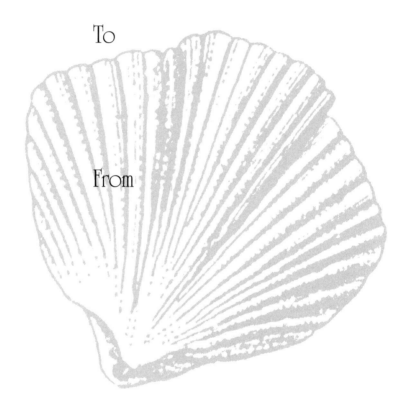

From

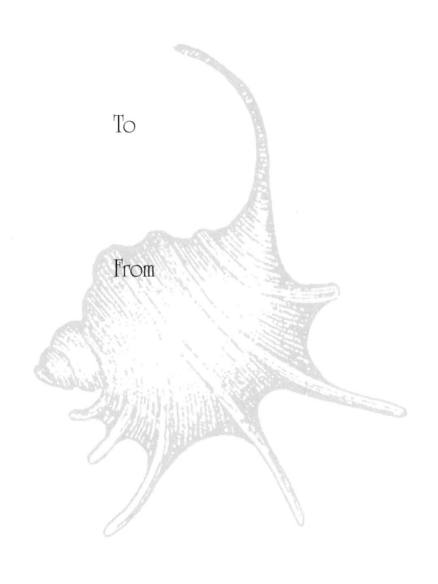

To

From

2199 Keep for your records

Message in a Book

By Michelle Patrizio
ISBN: 0-89716-839-9
Peanut Butter Publishing
212 - 1656 Duranleau Street
Granville Island, Vancouver, B.C.
Canada V6H 3S4

When Peanut Butter receives this book, it will be sent back to you.
Your name will not be passed on to any other organization.

Your Name (please print clearly):

_____

Your Address: _____

_____

City: _____

Province/State: _____

Postal/Zip Code: _____

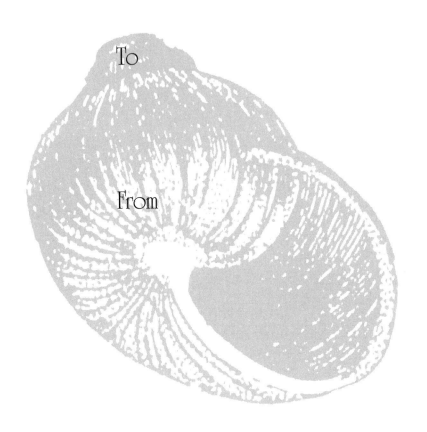

To

From

To

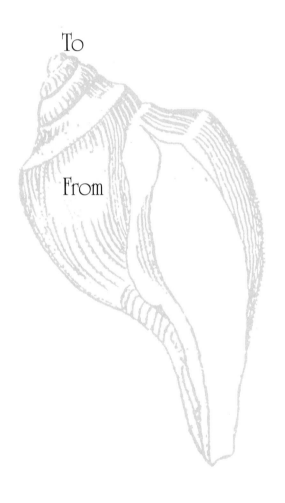

From

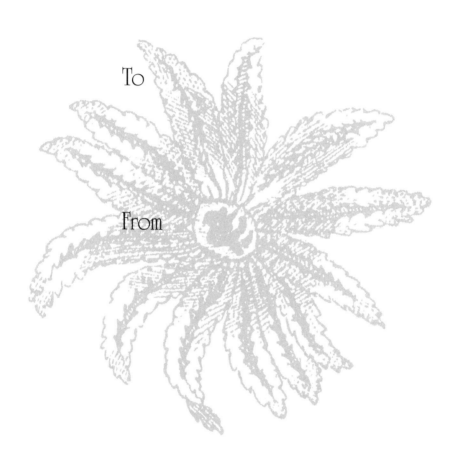

To

From

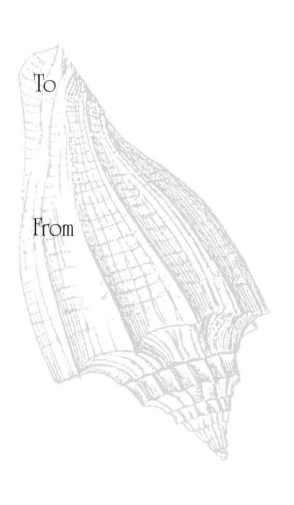

To

From

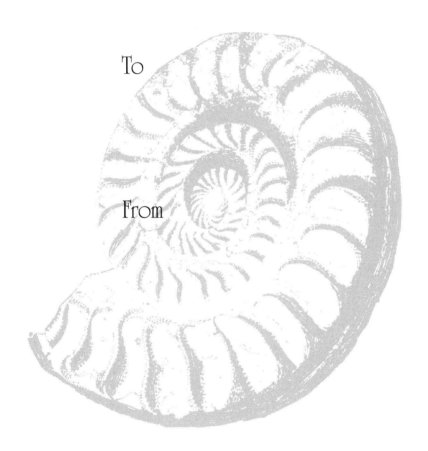

To

From

To

From

To

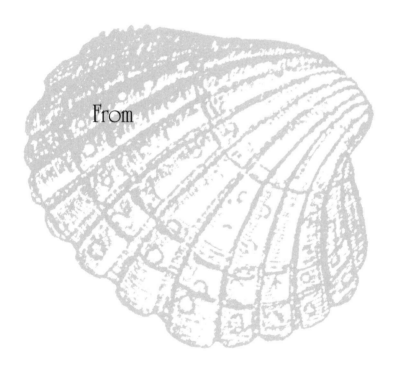

From

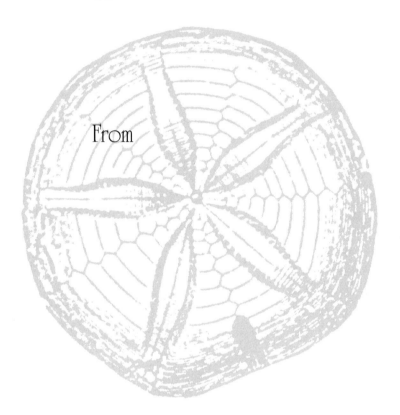

To

From

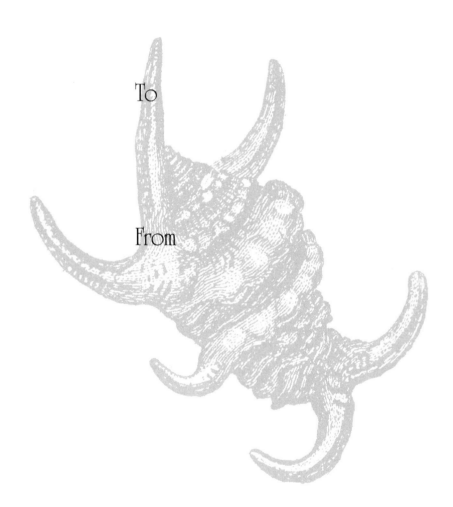

To

From

To

From

To

From

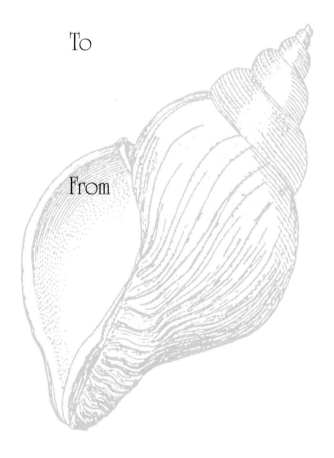

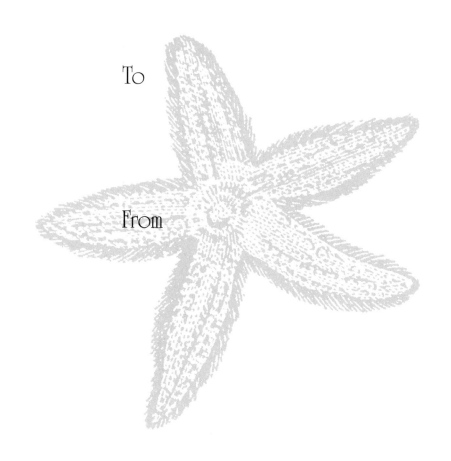

To

From

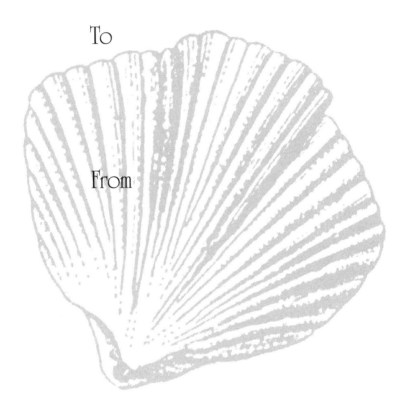

To

From

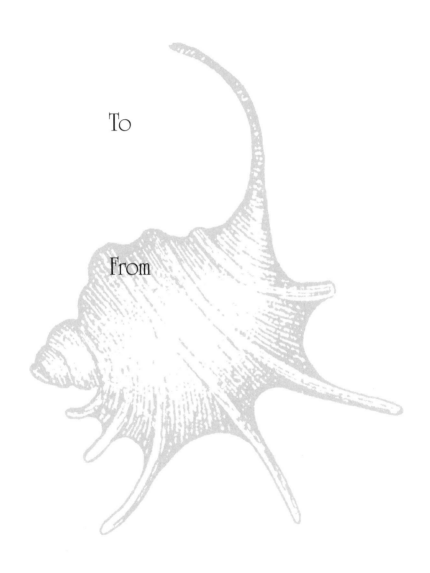

To

From

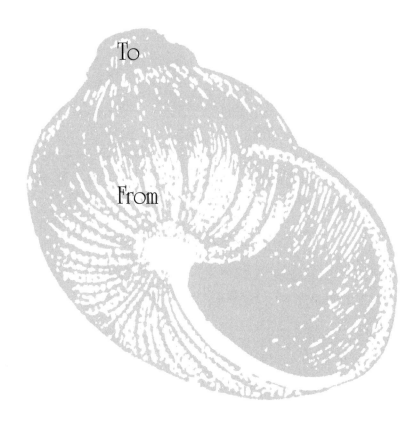

To

From

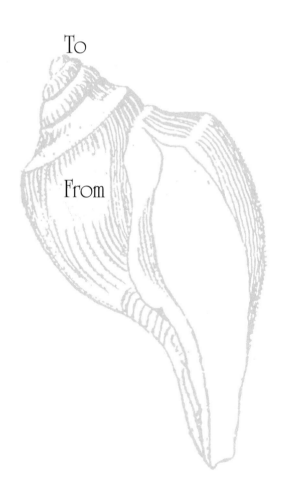

To

From

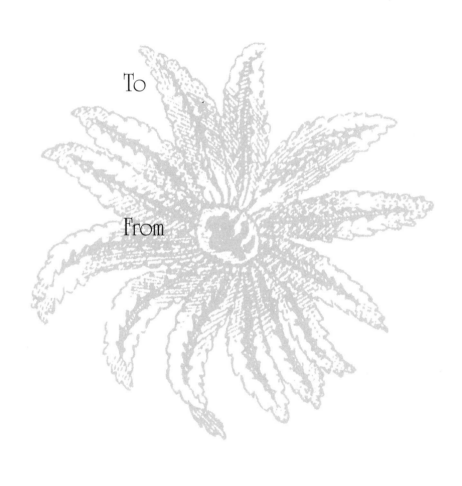

To

From

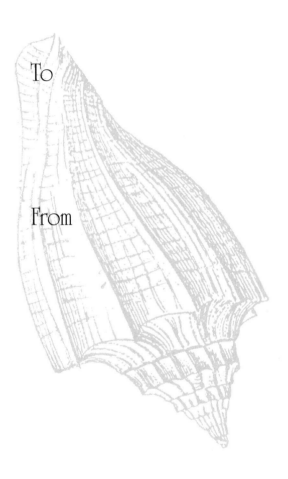

To

From

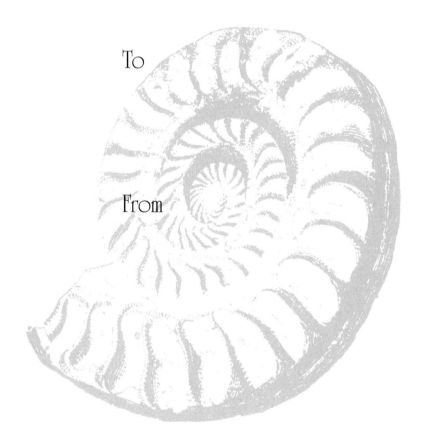

To

From

To

From

To

From

To

From

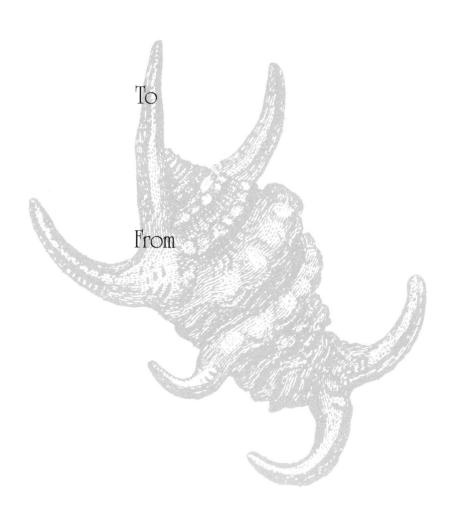

To

From

To

From

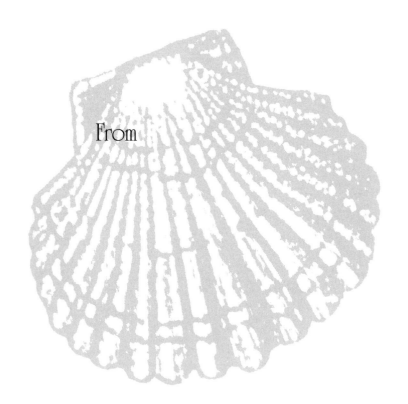

To

From

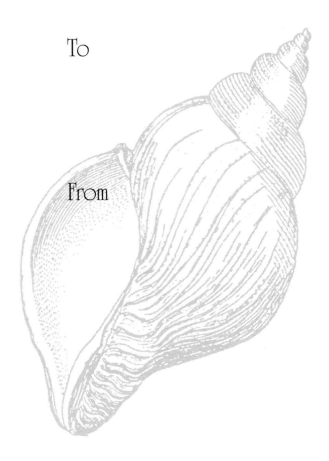

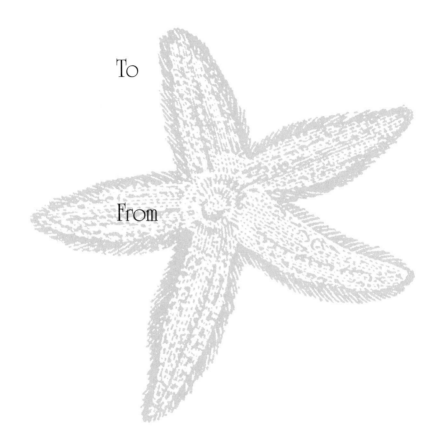

To

From

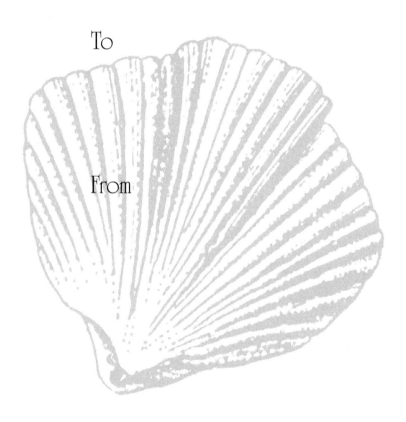

To

From

To

From

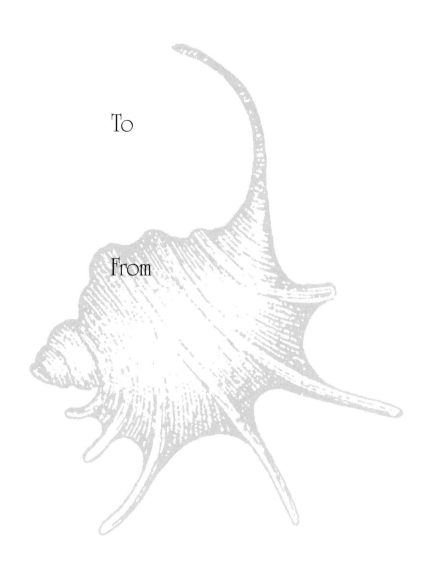

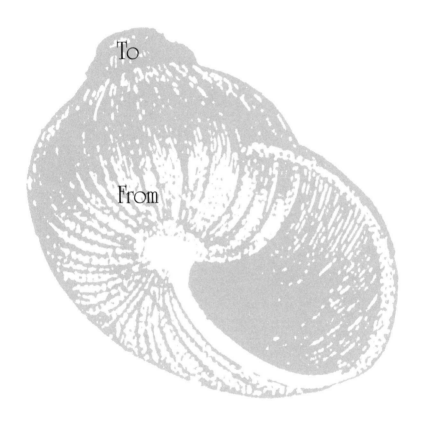

To

From

To

From

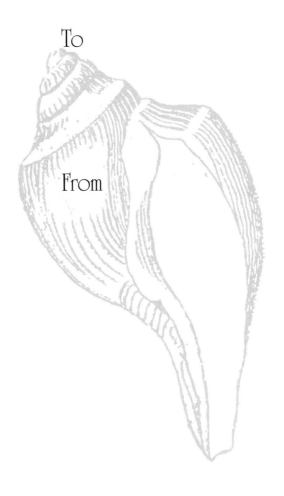

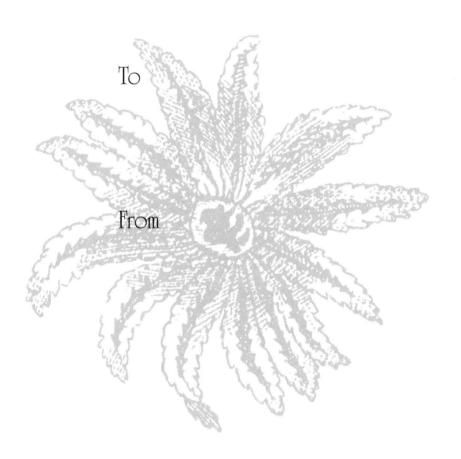

To

From

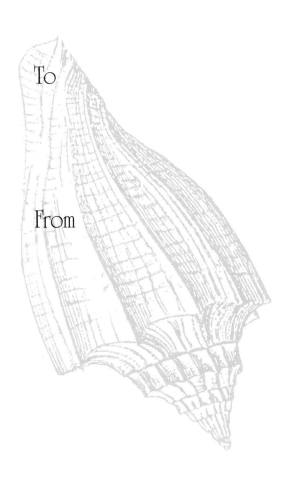

To

From

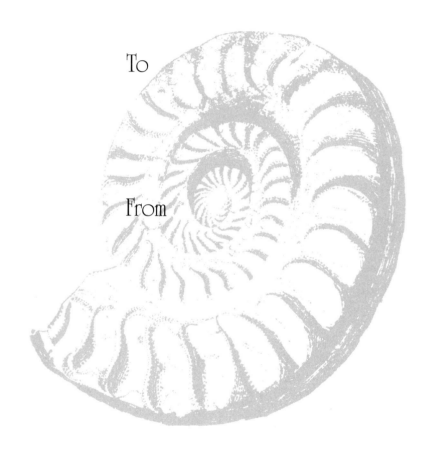

To

From

To

From

To

From

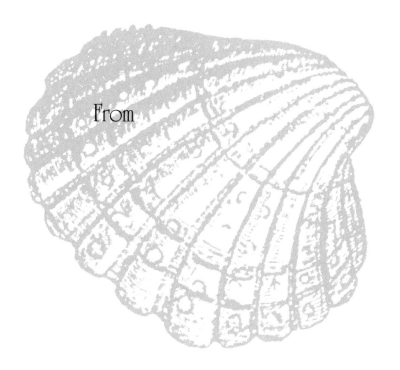

To

From

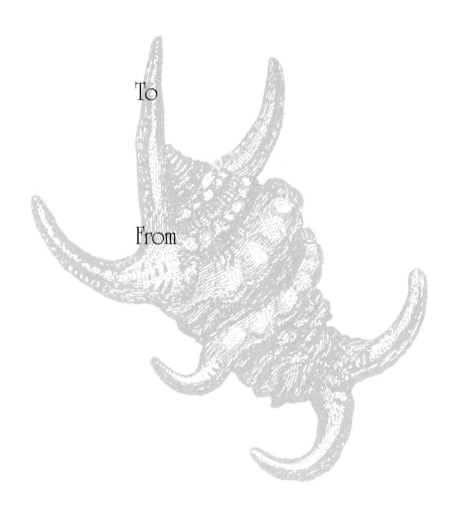

To

From

To

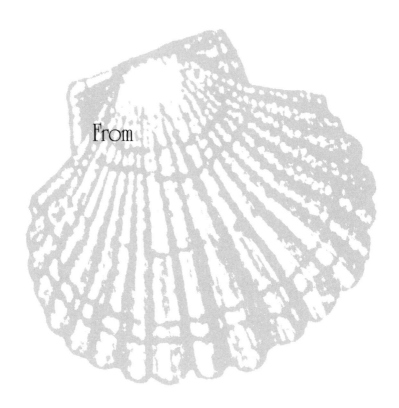

From

If you are the last person
to receive this book …

If you are the last person to receive this book, you have a delightful and important role to play in completing the circle. Kindly mail the book back to Peanut Butter Publishing, who will return it to the original owner. If this should pose a problem for you, please contact Peanut Butter. We will be happy to help.

Thank you very much.

Peanut Butter Publishing
#212 - 1656 Duranleau Street
Granville Island, Vancouver, B.C.
Canada V6H 3S4
Tel: 604-688-0320
Email: pnutpubv@axion.net

ORDER FORM

If you wish to order more copies, please photocopy this page.

Message in a Book

is also available from your local bookstore or gift shop.

CANADIAN FUNDS		U.S. FUNDS	
___ Copies @ $19.95 $_____		___ Copies @ $14.95 $_____	
GST (7%) $_____			
Shipping (1st book) $ 6.00		Shipping (1st book) $ 4.00	
Add $4 for each		Add $3 for each	
additional book $_____		additional book $_____	
Total enclosed $_____		Total enclosed $_____	

Make cheque or money order payable to:

Peanut Butter Publishing

Your Name _____

Your Address _____

City, Province/State _____

Postal/Zip Code _____

Phone (work) _____ (home) _____

PEANUT BUTTER PUBLISHING
Suite 212 - 1656 Duranleau Street • Granville Island
• Vancouver, B.C. • Canada • V6H 3S4 • 604-688-0320 •
email: pnutpubv@axion.net
Internet: http://www.pbpublishing.com

Printed in Canada

Thank you for your order!